Author:
Fiona Macdonald studied history at Cambridge University, England, and at the University of East Anglia. She has taught in schools, adult education centers, and universities, and is the author of numerous books for children on historical topics.

Artist:
David Antram was born in Brighton, England, in 1958. He studied at Eastbourne College of Art and then worked in advertising for 15 years before becoming a full-time artist. He has illustrated many children's nonfiction books.

Series creator:
David Salariya was born in Dundee, Scotland. He has illustrated a wide range of books and has created and designed many new series for publishers in the UK and overseas. David established The Salariya Book Company in 1989. He lives in Brighton with his wife, illustrator Shirley Willis, and their son, Jonathan.

Editor: **Tanya Kant**

Editorial Assistant: **Mark Williams**

PAPER FROM
SUSTAINABLE
FORESTS

© The Salariya Book Company Ltd MMX
No part of this publication may be reproduced in whole or in part, or stored in a retrieval system, or transmitted in any form or by any means, electronic, mechanical, photocopying, recording, or otherwise, without written permission of the publisher. For information regarding permission, write to the copyright holder.

Published in Great Britain in 2010 by
The Salariya Book Company Ltd
25 Marlborough Place, Brighton BN1 1UB

ISBN-13: 978-0-531-20473-3 (lib. bdg.) 978-0-531-22828-9 (pbk.)
ISBN-10: 0-531-20473-1 (lib. bdg.) 0-531-22828-2 (pbk.)

All rights reserved.
Published in 2010 in the United States
by Franklin Watts
An imprint of Scholastic Inc.
557 Broadway, New York, NY 10012
Published simultaneously in Canada.

A CIP catalog record for this book is available
from the Library of Congress.

Printed and bound in Heshan, China.
Printed on paper from sustainable sources.
1 2 3 4 5 6 7 8 9 10 R 18 17 16 15 14 13 12 11 10 09

You Wouldn't Want to Be Joan of Arc!

A Mission You Might Want to Miss

Written by
Fiona Macdonald

Illustrated by
David Antram

Created and designed by
David Salariya

Franklin Watts®
An Imprint of Scholastic Inc.
NEW YORK • TORONTO • LONDON • AUCKLAND • SYDNEY
MEXICO CITY • NEW DELHI • HONG KONG
DANBURY, CONNECTICUT

Contents

Introduction

The year? It's 1428. The place? Domrémy, a village in northeast France. And you? You're Joan, the daughter of peasant farmers. Your family is neither very rich nor very poor. Like all the other local youngsters, you've grown up living in fear. For years, war has been raging throughout France. One of your cousins has been killed in battle, and the village church—next door to your family's house—has been burned down by the enemy. So far, you've managed to stay safe. But you face great dangers ahead. Why? Because you dream of a secret, sacred mission: to rescue France from its attackers!

You're young—just 16. You're not a famous or powerful person. You can't read or write, and you haven't been trained to use weapons. You don't understand politics or know how to plan a battle. But you're utterly convinced that you must save your country. How can you fulfill your dream?

I have a mission! But how can a girl like me save an entire country?

Dutiful Daughter

Your parents are respectable and hardworking. Your father keeps sheep and grows crops; your mother cooks, sews, cleans, and looks after the household. You're from a large family! You have a sister and three brothers, all older than you. For as long as you can remember, everyone has assumed that you'll grow up to be like them: busy, helpful, and stay-at-home.

Your parents—and the Catholic Church—say that, as a girl, you must be modest, gentle, and obedient. They expect you to marry one day and become a dutiful wife and mother.

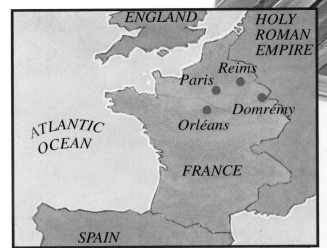

YOUR HOME is in the village of Domrémy, in the region of Lorraine. It's good farming country, with vineyards on the hillsides and rich green pastures beside the wide Meuse River.

A Good Girl

ALONG WITH most people in Europe at this time, you've been brought up as a Catholic. Local priests and your mother have taught you to say prayers.

YOU HAVE LEARNED sewing and spinning so that you can make clothes and household linens. You're proud of these skills.

TO SHOW YOUR FAITH, you make garlands of flowers to decorate holy statues.

In the War Zone

You cannot remember a time without war. In fact, there has been fighting between England and France for almost a century. This conflict will come to be known as the Hundred Years' War. Most of the battles have been fought on French soil. Hundreds of peaceful villages have been attacked, and countless families have seen their farms ruined. Vast areas of the countryside are now poor.

Your village is right between lands ruled by sworn enemies—the king of France and the duke of Burgundy (who is friendly with the English). Earlier this year, you and your family had to run for your lives when Burgundian soldiers attacked. You hid for two weeks in a nearby town, until it was safe to return.

WAR HERO? The English still boast about their brave King Henry V. In 1415, he won a famous victory against the king of France at the Battle of Agincourt. But six years ago, he died of dysentery at the age of 35. Now his little son is king of England—and claims to be king of France, too.

God help us!

8

Henry V, former king of England

I'm dead famous in England, you know.

Who ordered takeout?

Handy Hint

Don't be brave! If enemies attack, don't try to fight back. Just run away and hide. With luck, you might survive.

GREEDY LOOTERS. Invading troops will steal everything they can carry. If you have animals, they'll cook and eat them!

ANGRY ATTACKERS. Rough soldiers will threaten women and children. Stay out of their way if you can!

CRUEL DESTROYERS. Before marching on, enemies will set fire to houses, farms, and barns, leaving villagers homeless.

Rival Rulers

Your beloved homeland is in danger. For the past 90 years, English kings have been invading France. They claim they have the right to rule France because their family is descended from a French princess.

The leadership of France has been too disorganized to stop the English. In 1392, King Charles VI of France went insane. Since then, his royal relatives have struggled with each other for power. During all this chaos, the English have conquered half of France.

The Story So Far:

1. CONFUSED KING. King Charles VI has a nickname—Charles the Mad. For many years, the poor king did not know who he was. Sometimes, he thought he was made of glass!

I'm his brother!

I'm feeling rather fragile today...

4. LEFT IN CHARGE. By 1417, Charles VI was too ill to rule France. His 14-year-old son, Prince Charles, took over the government. At first, he was helped by the duke of Burgundy.

Paris

English lands

Charles's land

5. THE ROYAL RIVALRIES continued for years. In 1419, Prince Charles's royal friends murdered the duke of Burgundy. This made the Burgundians hate the French royals—and ally with the English.

6. FRANCE is now a divided country. Charles VII, England, and Burgundy each control different areas.

2. THE ROYAL FAMILY could not agree who should rule France while Charles VI was ill. Charles's brother, Prince Louis of Orléans, quarreled with Charles's cousin, the duke of Burgundy.

Handy Hint

Don't trust your neighbors! The outskirts of your village, just across the river, have been conquered by the Burgundians.

The king is not fit to rule! I should be in control!

Well, I'm his favorite cousin!

3. IN 1407, the duke of Burgundy ordered the murder of Prince Louis of Orléans. This made French royals hate the Burgundians.

Burgundian lands

7. FRENCH ROYAL TROOPS are depressed and disorganized. How can they compete with armored English knights on horseback or archers firing longbows, England's deadliest weapon?

8. CHARLES VII became king of France at the age of 19 and has been in power for six years—but he's still in great danger.

Hearing Voices

As a child, you did not understand the causes of the war that was wrecking your homeland. You just went on with your life, helping your mother around the house and taking care of the farm animals. Then, one day, about four years ago, something extraordinary happened....

You were by yourself, in your father's garden, when suddenly, there were voices! They held you spellbound with their sweetness and power. You looked everywhere, but there was no one to be seen—just dazzling light from the sun. Then the voices stopped, and the sun's rays dimmed. Confused, frightened, and awestruck, you ran home, crying.

Handy Hint

Don't tell anyone! The church and the villagers are suspicious of people who claim to see visions or hear voices. They might say you're crazy— or a witch!

Who Do the Voices Belong To?

AT FIRST, you don't know who spoke to you. But during the next four years, you hear the voices again—many, many times. At last, you think you recognize them:

SAINT CATHERINE of Alexandria (below). A wise and holy young woman, she was killed for being a Christian. She is said to help people in danger.

SAINT MARGARET of Antioch. She was also killed for being a Christian, and is said to help women during childbirth. Legends tell how she escaped unharmed from the belly of a dragon!

SAINT MICHAEL. Prince of angels and a mighty warrior, he is believed to protect the French army.

An Urgent Mission

You're a sincere Catholic. You've always tried to follow church teachings—and obey your parents, too. But now, in 1428, you're about to horrify—and frighten—everyone who loves you. Why, Joan, why? You say that your voices are telling you to take action. You must obey them—it's a holy command!

You, Joan, a 16-year-old peasant girl, must leave home and lead an army to defeat the English. You're also to take young King Charles VII to the ancient royal city of Reims, which has been under English control since Charles became king. There, Charles can be blessed by the church and officially crowned king of France, like all his royal ancestors. This will prove that God wants him to be king.

YOUR VOICES are very precious to you—and, at first, rather worrisome. So you keep what you've heard to yourself and never repeat it to anyone.

Can I really lead an army?

14

Who does she think she is?

Handy Hint

Stick to your nickname! It's *La Pucelle* ("The Maiden"), and it might protect you. It means that you are holier than other women, a bit like a nun.

SOME PEOPLE don't think that you or your voices are holy. These folks believe in a sinister pagan prophecy that says that a "maiden from the oakwoods" (the French countryside) will one day save France. Are you that maiden? If so, you're extremely dangerous!

Why You?

HOURS OF PRAYER have convinced you that the voices you hear come from heaven. You feel sure that God approves of your plan. But will anyone else believe you? And why have you been given this difficult and dangerous task?

Joan is a pagan! She's the maiden from the oakwoods!

Royal Meeting

Your mind is made up. You must go to the royal court! But girls cannot travel alone, so you ask a male relative to ride with you. French soldiers are suspicious and send you back home, but you keep trying. At last, two French nobles take you to the king. They think you might be useful.

In 1429, you kneel before young Charles VII and beg him to let you help France. King Charles looks worried and alarmed. Who are you? Can he trust you? He sends you to be questioned by church lawyers. They think you are honest and trustworthy—so Charles lets you join his army!

Poor Charles needs all the help he can get. They say he has only four gold coins left.

16

ARMED WITH A BANNER. You want to fight with a banner (a sign of leadership) instead of a sword. Charles gives you a holy banner, decorated with a picture of Jesus Christ and two angels. You're also given a suit of armor to protect you.

Handy Hint

Travel in disguise. Dress as a servant boy for your journey. That way, the rough, rude soldiers will be less likely to pick on you!

Ihesvs Maria

BEST BEHAVIOR. You purify the French army by sending the soldiers' girlfriends home and making the men say their prayers.

Saving a City

To have a hope of ruling France, young King Charles must keep the city of Orléans under his rule. If the English conquer Orléans, they'll soon control all of France—including the rich Loire Valley, called the "Garden of France."

Can Orléans Survive an English Siege?

SOLDIERS DEFENDING the walls of Orléans are in great danger, but they must keep watch in case of an attack.

English soldiers have surrounded Orléans, trapping its citizens inside the city walls. The city's food and water supplies are running low, and disease is spreading. English troops have also captured the twin towers that guard Orléans's main gate. You've been wounded, but your troops need you. You must stop the English from breaking into the city and killing its inhabitants.

Handy Hint

Surprise the enemy! Tell your soldiers to sail down the river and attack the English from behind.

WAR CAMP. English troops set up camp beside the city, so that they are always close by, ready to attack.

SHARPSHOOTERS. English archers fire arrows at defenders who dare to look over the battlements.

WRECKED. English armies have burned the local countryside, so there is little food for Orléans's inhabitants.

COMMAND AND CONTROL. For safety, English officers give orders from a nearby monastery.

FIREPOWER. Huge stone balls, fired from English cannons, can smash city gates.

LOOK OUT! English patrols stop Orléans's citizens from sending for help or trying to escape.

POISON WATER. English soldiers have polluted nearby wells, so Orléans's defenders can't get fresh water.

The King Is Crowned

With you to lead and inspire them, the French army saves Orléans. King Charles VII is extremely grateful, but his enemies are furious, his courtiers are astonished, and church leaders are suspicious. How can French soldiers be commanded by a girl with no army training? How on earth did you lead them to victory?

Don't let cruel words worry you. Your next task is to lead Charles's army through lands controlled by the English to the city of Reims. There, Charles VII can be crowned at last, like all his ancestors. Coronation is an ancient, holy ceremony. The church teaches that it turns a king into a ruler blessed, approved, and guided by God. Until the coronation, many people will say that Charles is not a real king.

Marching to Reims

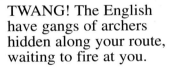

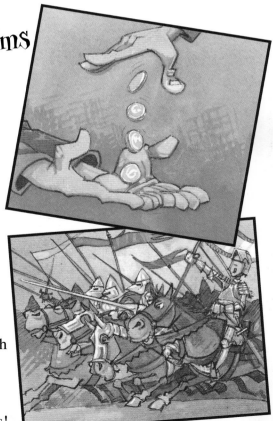

TWANG! The English have gangs of archers hidden along your route, waiting to fire at you.

CLINK! England has paid Burgundy to recruit more men to fight against you.

CRASH! You are hit by a stone thrown by an English soldier. You must stagger to your feet and continue.

CHARGE! An English army tries to block your path, but your soldiers attack and scatter them. Then you march into Reims!

Isabeau, queen of France, has had a tragic life. Her husband, Charles VI, was mentally ill and most of her 12 children died. In desperation, she allied with the Burgundians and agreed with them that England should rule France. To back England's claim, she may even have spread rumors that her son, Charles VII, was not her husband's child.

Handy Hint

Graciously accept the praise showered on you by the French. Give thanks to God that you've made it to Reims. This is the happiest day of your life!

Mission accomplished!

21

Sensing Doom

It's winter, 1429. Your leg has been badly injured by a crossbow bolt. Your men have won a few small battles, but Paris, the French capital, is still under English control. King Charles VII's advisers are trying—but failing—to make peace with Burgundy. They want to make sure that Charles keeps control of the lands you won along the way to Reims.

It's too cold and muddy for the armies to fight, so you rest for a while. Your leg gets better, but you fear that you will soon be betrayed and captured. Your voices are warning that this will happen before St. John's Day (June 24) in 1430.

1. SURROUNDED! On May 23, 1430, your soldiers are attacked by the Burgundians. You are cut off during the retreat and surrounded.

Grab the girl!

It's all your fault!

4. SQUABBLE, SQUABBLE. Charles VII's inexperienced courtiers bicker among themselves, accusing each other of betraying you. In fact, it was their bad military advice that put you in danger.

5. RANSOM! Charles VII offers a ransom (a rich reward) for setting you free. The Burgundians refuse and sell you to the English for 10,000 gold coins.

2. CAPTURED! The soldiers drag you off your horse and take you to their leader, Lionel of Wandomme.

You're coming with us!

Handy Hint

In jail, wear boys' clothes! The soldiers will be less likely to attack you. Trousers are also warmer in a damp, drafty cell.

3. HOORAY! The Burgundians rejoice at your capture, while your French soldiers are devastated.

Woo-hoo!

It's payback time.

6. DESPERATE! You try to escape by jumping from a tower that's 70 feet (20 meters) high. You land in a muddy moat. You're injured, but you survive.

7. IN CHAINS. You are locked in an army prison and surrounded by rough soldiers. As a girl, you ought to have women jailers, but the English want you to suffer.

23

A Terrifying Trial

The English want revenge! You have stopped them from completing their conquest of France, by making sure that Charles VII has been crowned king instead of his English rival. Angry English soldiers take you to Rouen in northwest France, a city they control. There are clear rules, respected by both the English and French, for dealing with captured enemies. Usually, important prisoners like you are ransomed and then set free. But the English want you to be punished as severely as possible. They accuse you of breaking the Catholic Church's holy laws—a very serious crime. Your trial, in a church court, begins in February 1431. It's a cruel farce.

Forced Confession

The court finds you guilty—of course! After the trial, you are forced to sign a "confession" that you cannot read and do not really understand. It says that you have broken church laws, that you have asked the church to forgive you, and that you promise to never do wrong again.

What am I signing?

The judge and lawyers all support England. They are too frightened—or greedy—to treat you fairly.

The English accuse you of witchcraft—a deadly sin. They declare that your voices are devils, not saints.

The church lawyers claim that your male clothes are evil, unnatural, and against God's laws.

Handy Hint

Beware! The lawyers will try to trap you into saying something sinful. Think carefully before you answer!

There are no witnesses to speak up for you, and no French lawyers to defend you.

You ask the court to write to the pope (the head of the Catholic Church) and ask for a fair trial. Your request is denied.

Life – or Death?

The English are delighted you were found guilty—but furious that you were not put to death. Because you confessed, the church will give you a chance to reform—though you'll spend the rest of your life in jail. You'll have to stop meddling in politics, believing that you hear voices, and wearing men's clothes. It's all part of your punishment.

You try to obey the court, but it's impossible! You can't ignore your voices; you hear them every day. And you go back to wearing men's clothes after a male prisoner attacks you. (You ask for a woman guard, but the English refuse.) This means you've broken church laws for a second time. Your fate is sealed— you must die!

Glorious Memory

You are burned at the stake on May 30, 1431, holding a little cross handed to you by a kindly peasant. You are just 19 years old. You have suffered a grave injustice and a terrible death. But your short life has changed the course of history. For a while, the English will try to make everyone forget about you. But in 1449, they will be driven out of Rouen. The long war will be over at last, and France will be at peace.

Soon after, the church will look back with horror at your trial and declare that you should never have been killed. It will call you a holy martyr—and a saint.

Still Honored!

YOU HAVE SHOWN what an ordinary young woman can achieve. Tourists visit your home at Domrémy to show respect.

Handy Hint

Follow Joan's example! Speak out for what you believe in.

IN 1920, you were made a saint by Pope Benedict XV. Catholics say you perform miracles to guide, help, and heal.

YOUR STORY has inspired great paintings, statues, films, plays, and poems.

IN FRANCE, you are a national hero and a proud symbol of independence.

JOAN'S VOICES. Today, many people doubt that Joan really heard the voices of saints.

But Joan—and her supporters— certainly believed she did, and some modern-day Christians believe so, too.

29

Glossary

battlement A wall at the top of a castle that has narrow spaces built into it for shooting at enemies.

bolt A sharp metal spike, like a short arrow. Bolts are fired from a crossbow—a short, mechanical bow that's fired with a trigger.

Burgundy During Joan of Arc's lifetime, a dukedom in Europe that included parts of modern-day France and Switzerland.

coronation An official ceremony to crown a monarch and declare him or her to be the kingdom's head of state.

courtier A member of the royal court who advised or entertained the king or queen.

damned A religious expression meaning that someone will go to hell after death.

dysentery A disease that causes severe diarrhea and can result in death if left untreated.

farce A ridiculous or pointless event, such as a trial for a person whom the court is already determined to find guilty.

heir The person who will inherit a kingdom when the current monarch dies.

Hundred Years' War A series of wars, fought between England, France, and Burgundy, for the right to rule France. The fighting lasted for 116 years, from 1337 to 1453.

longbow The most important weapon used by English foot soldiers during Joan of Arc's time. The bow was about 6 feet (2 m) long and made of tough, springy wood. It could fire an arrow more than 100 yards.

martyr A person who is killed for promoting or defending his or her religious beliefs.

miracle An event that witnesses believe was the result of a supernatural power.

monastery A place where Catholic monks live and work. In Joan of Arc's time, monasteries were centers of art and learning; some also housed hospitals.

pagan To the Christians of Joan of Arc's time, a person who followed a religion other than Christianity.

peasant In Joan of Arc's time, a member of the social class that farmed the countryside.

pope The leader of the Roman Catholic Church.

prophecy A statement that claims to predict the future.

ransom A large sum of money paid to enemies to set a war prisoner free. In Joan of Arc's time, rich prisoners were usually set free after their families paid a ransom. Poor prisoners, whose families could not afford to pay, were often killed.

saint A dead person honored for living a holy life devoted to Christianity. Some Christians believe that saints perform miracles to help the living.

siege An attempt to conquer a walled city or fortress over a long period of time. The attackers can win a siege by breaking into the city or by wearing down the enemy through a lack of food or water.

spinning Twisting animal hair (wool) or plant fibers (flax) to make a strong, smooth thread for weaving or sewing.

vision An experience caused by a supernatural force.

Index